D0567920

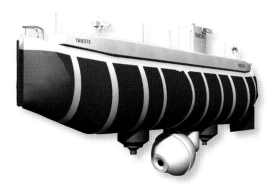

өDiscovery
EDUCATION™

Published in 2014 by The Rosen Publishing Group, Inc.
29 East 21st Street, New York, NY 10010

Photo Credits: **KEY** tl=top left; tc=top center; tr=top right; cl=center; br=bottom right; bg=background

CBT = Corbis; DT = Dreamstime; iS = istockphoto.com; SH = Shutterstock; SP = SeaPics; TF = Topfoto; TPL = photolibrary.com; wiki = Wikipedia

6–7bg SP; **9**c iS; **12**bc, cl TPL; **13**bl TPL; **18**cr CBT; tl DT; cl TPL; **19**tl, tr CBT; bc SH; **24**bl, cl, cr, tr CBT; br TPL; **26**bl TF; **27**cr TPL; tc wiki; **28**br, cl SH; **29**c CBT; **30–31**bg iS

All illustrations copyright Weldon Owen Pty Ltd

Weldon Owen Pty Ltd

Managing Director: Kay Scarlett
Creative Director: Sue Burk
Publisher: Helen Bateman
Senior Vice President, International Sales: Stuart Laurence
Vice President Sales North America: Ellen Towell
Administration Manager, International Sales: Kristine Ravn

Library of Congress Cataloging-in-Publication Data

Sheehan, Robert.
 The undersea lab : exploring the oceans / by Robert Sheehan.
    pages cm. — (Discovery education: earth and space science)
 Includes index.
 ISBN 978-1-4777-6166-3 (library) — ISBN 978-1-4777-6168-7 (pbk.) —
 ISBN 978-1-4777-6169-4 (6-pack)
 1. Oceanographic research stations—Juvenile literature. 2. Underwater exploration—Juvenile literature. I. Title.
 GC57.S463 2014
 551.46072—dc23
 5418 3230 8/14   2013023327

Manufactured in the United States of America

CPSIA Compliance Information: Batch #W14PK2: For Further Information contact Rosen Publishing, New York, New York at 1-800-237-9932

EARTH AND SPACE SCIENCE

THE UNDERSEA LAB
EXPLORING THE OCEANS

ROBERT SHEEHAN

Contents

The Ocean 6

The Power of Earth's Oceans 8

The Sunlight Zone 10

In Deep Water 12

The Seafloor 14

Disturbances on the Ocean Floor 16

Ocean Pollution..................................18

Earth's Climate and the Oceans..........20

Climate Change and
    the World's Oceans 22

Marine Scientists 24

Undersea Technology 26

A Healthy Planet.................................28

Glossary...30

Index 32

Websites...32

The Ocean

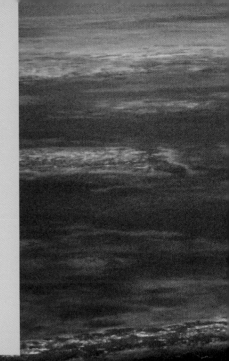

Planet Earth looks blue when viewed from space because the ocean is Earth's largest domain. Water covers more than 70 percent of Earth's surface and almost all of this is salt water in the oceans.

The largest and perhaps strangest creatures live in the ocean. There are hundreds of thousands of known marine species, living mostly near or within the seafloor, and more unknown species waiting to be discovered. The ocean's surface waters absorb the Sun's heat and influence Earth's climate. Microscopic ocean life uses the Sun's energy to make oxygen. The ocean, which most likely gave rise to life on Earth, now sustains it.

Icebergs afloat
Made of compressed snow, freshwater icebergs break off from ice shelves in polar regions, and their location is monitored worldwide. The density of ice is less than seawater, so icebergs float with only about 10 percent above water level. The surface above can be more than 1,000 square miles (259,000 ha) in area.

Abundant growth

The top 660 feet (200 m) of the ocean's waters are penetrated by enough sunlight to allow photosynthesis. This process allows abundant growth of marine plant and animal life. The tiniest phytoplankton thrive, as do fish of various sizes, warm-blooded mammals, and a variety of other species.

Colorful life

Corals are small animals that live in vast colonies, usually in warm waters. They feed on tiny organisms, and most need sunlight to grow. Corals secrete a form of calcium that hardens to form brightly colored protective skeletons. They also provide a home for a large variety of marine life.

Coral atoll

Volcanoes are spread around the world, but around 90 percent of volcanic activity occurs in the ocean. Many ocean volcanoes slowly sink as they get older. Coral grows around the edges of the sinking land. After hundreds of thousands of years, a coral reef ring, or atoll, encloses a shallow central lagoon.

The Power of Earth's Oceans

Ocean waters are continuously moving, affected by air pressure, temperature, density, and gravity. Variations create upwelling and downwelling currents. The energy contained within such large moving masses has the potential to be both constructive and destructive. The constant motion of the ocean tides and waves is demonstration of its power. Ongoing scientific research is looking at finding ways to economically convert more of this power into electrical energy.

Underwater movements of Earth's crust and extreme low-pressure atmospheric systems are both capable of causing seawater to flood coastal land. The 2004 Asian tsunami and Hurricane Katrina in 2005 are recent examples of the destructive power of the ocean.

Formation of a tsunami
Earth's rigid, outermost crust is divided into slowly moving plates that can push too hard against each other. A sudden slip underwater causes major disturbance at the plate boundary. Ocean swells then radiate from the site.

Shock waves
Sudden seafloor disruptions send out powerful shock waves but cause relatively minor surface changes in deep, ocean water. The swell is hardly noticed by sailors as the shock waves move beneath the surface.

Closer to shore
Approaching the shore with decreased speed, the swells become waves of increasing height and frequency. The tsunami arrives as a series of high crests and deep troughs.

Friction against the seafloor at the base of the wave slows its movement. When the wave's face becomes too steep, its peak falls forward and can curl over a pocket of air, crashing down with considerable force.

Power generation

The ocean is a valuable renewable resource for at least three types of electrical power generation. Tidal and wave power generators convert the movement, or kinetic energy, of ocean waters into electrical power. Thermal energy generators convert the heat energy of ocean surface waters.

The Sunlight Zone

The process of photosynthesis occurs all over planet Earth, including within the upper two percent of the ocean, known as the sunlight zone. Microscopic plants called phytoplankton convert the Sun's energy into chemical energy in the form of rich glucose. This process uses carbon dioxide and produces oxygen. Healthy phytoplankton swarms give off a dull, red glow that can be seen in satellite photographs. As a result, any sites that have unhealthy phytoplankton growth can be identified and investigated.

Phytoplankton
These are smallest members of the food chain, and most are only single-cell algae. Necessary for the health of the whole ocean, they need upwelling water to supply them with mineral nutrients from the ocean bottom.

Zooplankton
These are the smallest marine animals, and drift with the ocean's currents. Examples include krill, tiny shrimplike crustaceans, which are an important food source for many fish and mammals, including some whales.

Blue whale
Comblike bristles, called baleen plates, in the whale's mouth filter plankton from the seawater.

Mahi mahi
This fish makes a popular meal for humans.

Mola mola
Swimming close to the surface, this bony fish feeds on plankton.

Life in the sunlight zone
Fish and marine mammals of various sizes thrive in the sunlight zone. Humans are the ultimate predators of these animals. Commercial overfishing and the unintended trapping of marine mammals in huge trawling nets is endangering many species.

Fishing
Humans catch seafood to eat, but numbers must be monitored to prevent overfishing.

UNDERWATER ZONES

1 Sunlight zone
Blue and green light travel deepest through seawater. Only blue light travels to the bottom of the sunlight zone, about 660 feet (200 m).

2 Twilight zone
Some sunlight filters through to this zone, but not enough to sustain plant life.

3 Midnight zone
Between 3,300 feet (1,000 m) and 10,000 feet (3,000 m) lies the midnight zone. Some sea creatures living here can produce sporadic light using bioluminescence.

4 Abyssal zone
This is the near-freezing and pitch-black bottom layer of the ocean.

Bluefin tuna
Traveling in schools, this fish eats squid and small fish.

In Deep Water

Around 65 percent of Earth's surface is covered by ocean waters deeper than 660 feet (200 m). At this depth there is little light and no plant life. The average ocean depth is about 3,800 feet (1,200 m).

These dark, cold regions are difficult places to conduct scientific research and even more difficult to live in. At a depth of 3,300 feet (1,000 m), the water pressure is around 100 times greater than at sea level. The fish living here have strong-boned frames and many are blind. Some fish are bioluminescent, that is, have glowing organs, which they use to lure prey. Others hunt with their keen sense of smell and touch.

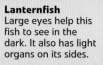

Lanternfish
Large eyes help this fish to see in the dark. It also has light organs on its sides.

Rattail fish
This fish gets its name from its long tail. It also has a large mouth and eyes.

Blue hake
Also known as hoki, this fish has a long body and good hearing.

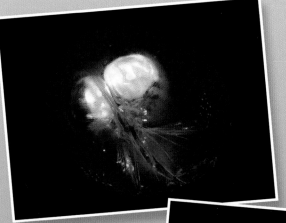

Giant ostracod
This crustacean grows to just over 1 inch (25 mm) in size. Ostracods probably use their bioluminescence as part of mating behavior.

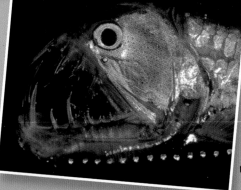

Viperfish
Typical of deep-sea fish, viperfish are small, up to 12 inches (30 cm) long, and have strong-boned frames. They wave a bioluminescent lure, then trap prey with their long teeth.

Glowing lure
The light at the end of the anglerfish's dorsal fin waves about to attract prey.

Did You Know?
Coral reefs also exist in deep, dark waters. They grow slowly and may live for more than 1,000 years. Their hard skeletons provide information about past climatic conditions.

Attached male
The tiny male anglerfish lives attached to the female's side.

Deep-sea anglerfish
With its fanglike teeth, this is one of the more odd-looking fish in the deep sea.

Tripod fish
This fish has a long tail and tail fins, allowing it to stand on the ocean floor.

Handle with care
Deep-sea species can die if they are captured and brought too quickly to the surface of the ocean from high-pressure depths. To avoid this, scientists have developed a pressurized fish trap that allows species to be studied at the surface of the ocean at high or gradually reducing pressure.

Sea cucumber
These creatures have adapted to darkness by having no eyes. They slowly and randomly sift through sediment on the ocean floor, looking for small algae and the remains of other marine life that settle to the bottom of the ocean.

The Seafloor

The formations of Earth's crust beneath the ocean are not unlike those of continents. There are plains, slopes, tall mountain ranges, and deep valleys known as trenches. Islands have risen from the ocean. Large areas of once dry land now form continental shelves.

The mid-ocean ridges are connected into a continuous underwater mountain range that circles the world. Flat plains extend at depths between 6,000 and 17,000 feet (1,800–5,200 m) from the ridges to the continental slopes.

Basin landmarks

Ocean basins are bounded by gently sloping continental slopes with abyssal plains forming the floor. Rising from the plains are conical volcanoes, seamounts, and flat-topped guyots, which are eroded volcanoes that were previously above sea level.

Continental shelf

Continental slope

Loading buoy and oil tanker

Crude oil reservoir

Oil is often found beneath continental shelves. Organic plant and animal material can become buried and trapped over millions of years. Increasing pressure and temperature convert this decayed material into the fossil fuel—crude oil.

Shales and porous rocks

Impermeable dense rock

Oil/water mix in pockets of porous rock

Non-porous rock

NATURAL GAS

Huge reservoirs of natural gas, mainly methane, are contained in seafloor sediments. Natural seepage from the trapped gas causes bubbles to rise. Gas is often held in solid crystalline structures, called methane hydrates. Scientists are investigating the properties and possible usefulness of these hydrates.

Bubbling methane gas

The volcanic mountains of Hawaii are considered Earth's tallest. From the seafloor, their height exceeds 31,000 feet (9,450 m).

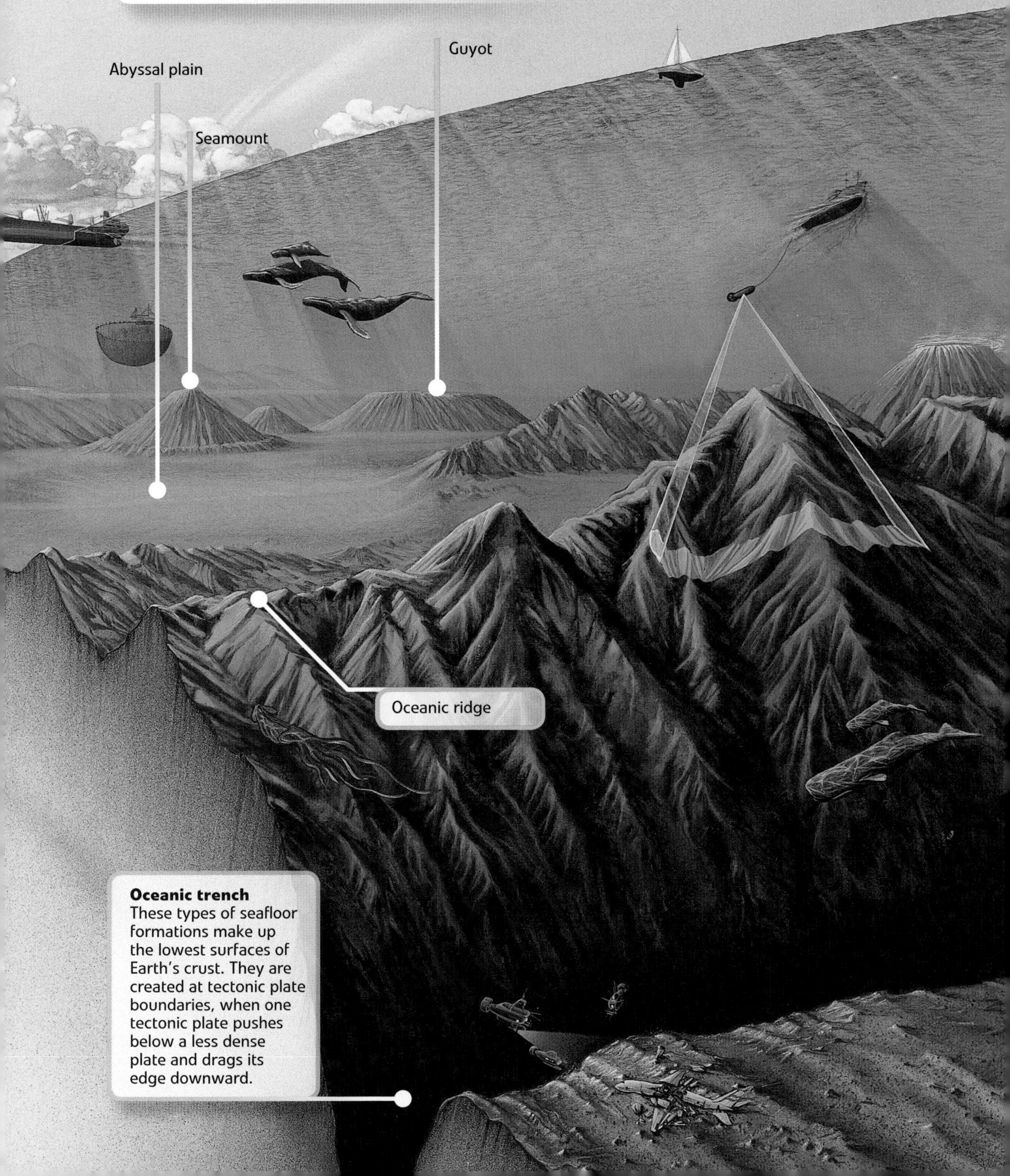

Abyssal plain

Seamount

Guyot

Oceanic ridge

Oceanic trench
These types of seafloor formations make up the lowest surfaces of Earth's crust. They are created at tectonic plate boundaries, when one tectonic plate pushes below a less dense plate and drags its edge downward.

Disturbances on the Ocean Floor

The ocean floor is the closest section of crust to Earth's hot and partially molten interior. Volcanic activity molds the contours of the ocean floor. Wherever weaknesses occur in the crust, superheated magma bursts through under pressure. This can occur at a single point, a volcanic cone, or along fissures many miles (km) in length.

The continual movement of tectonic plates also creates different seafloor features. Movements are usually only inches (cm) per year, but violent disturbances can occur when plates stick and then slip.

Convergent boundary
When plates collide and one subducts, this gives rise to trenches and volcanic activity.

Divergent boundary
Upwelling of the mantle occurs, which cools to form mid-ocean ridges.

Transform boundary
Sliding plates can cause severe seismic shocks if they stick together.

Terraces
Sometimes called hinge zones, these are steps along the walls of rift valleys.

Tectonic plates
Some heat rises from Earth's core to the surface by convection, an upward motion of the hot mantle rocks similar to the motion of boiling water. This drives movement of the surface tectonic plates. There are three general classes of movement at tectonic plate boundaries.

VENTING BLACK SMOKER

Cold seawater drops through cracks and is heated. Minerals dissolve in the superheated water under pressure. Sudden cooling of this fluid as it is forced back into the seawater through the chimney causes dissolved minerals to form tiny grains. These give the hydrothermal vent fluid its dark color. Chemical compounds of sulfur, carbon, and hydrogen allow bacteria to thrive, beginning a food chain that sustains a rich variety of life in the darkness.

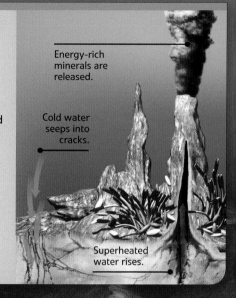

Energy-rich minerals are released.

Cold water seeps into cracks.

Superheated water rises.

Lava pillows
As escaping lava quickly cools, it forms piles of roundish rock blobs.

Exploration
Scientists use small manned submarines and remotely operated vehicles (ROVs).

Fiery fissure
Fissure vents are long but not very wide. They expel lava in a moderate manner.

Volcanic activity

Lava eruptions from fissures on the ocean floor occur only occasionally, but black smoker chimneys can remain active for decades and even centuries.

Ocean Pollution

Most of the time, we see evidence of pollution of the ocean's vast waters along continental coastlines. This environmental damage along shorelines is usually a result of human activity on land and spillages of oil at sea.

Other forms of pollution can go virtually unnoticed. The ocean absorbs higher quantities of atmospheric carbon dioxide and becomes more acidic. This acidification slows the growth rate of coral skeletons, which are home to many marine organisms.

Blue-green algae
Blooms of toxic bacteria or phytoplankton can pollute large ocean areas. They are harmful to most organisms. Other toxic pollutants, known as marine mucilage or mucus blobs, are increasing as oceans warm. They contain decaying organic material, bacteria, and viruses.

1 Plastic garbage on beach
Plastic, often manufactured with toxic additives, can take up to 400 years to decompose in the environment. Waste plastic is easily washed via storm water drains to beaches and the ocean.

2 Plastic floating in the sea
Lightweight plastic is transported long distances on fast-moving surface currents. The Great Pacific Garbage Patch, swirling clockwise around the North Pacific, consists mainly of plastic debris floating on and beneath the surface.

3 Plastic ingested by fish and birds
Plastic disintegrates to the microscopic level of zooplankton, where it enters the food chain. Pieces remain suspended in the water or settle to the bottom, polluting sediments. Larger pieces can block the digestive system of marine animals.

4 Humans eating fish
Toxic chemicals are entering the tissues of fish and other marine animals. Scientists are currently studying the effect of this on animals at the top of the marine food chain, particularly humans.

Leaking oil
Pollution of coastal waters and stretches of coastline by oil spills is big news. Unfortunately, aerial photographs of burning oil rigs or stranded tankers are familiar. Damage is mostly to coastal and estuarine environments and to local marine birds and animals.

Earth's Climate and the Oceans

A round 97 percent of global water is contained within the ocean. Some of this water evaporates, providing almost all rainfall on land as part of Earth's water cycle. The evaporation is caused by heat from the Sun. This heat is also exchanged between the ocean and Earth's atmosphere, controlling atmospheric circulation. The circulating winds, in turn, drive surface water currents, moving warmer water and air from the equatorial tropics toward the poles.

Hurricanes and severe tropical cyclones are low-pressure atmospheric systems that use heat stored in tropical oceans.

NORTH AMERICA

SOUTH AMERICA

The El Niño and La Niña effect

El Niño is part of a climate pattern where surface waters of the Pacific Ocean are warmer than usual. This results in weather disturbances, such as droughts. La Niña is the cold phase of the pattern, and often produces record snowfalls.

Peak El Niño
December–February

Peak La Niña
December–February

KEY

Dry and warm		Wet	
Warm		Wet and cool	
Dry		Cool	
Wet and warm		Dry and cool	

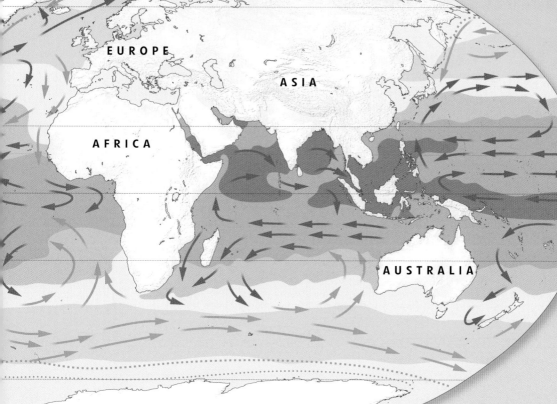

WATER TEMPERATURE

- ■ Above 86°F (30°C)
- ▨ 77–86°F (25–30°C)
- ▤ 68–77°F (20–25°C)
- □ 59–68°F (15–20°C)
- □ 50–59°F (10–15°C)
- □ 41–50°F (5–10°C)
- □ Under 41°F (5°C)
- •• Summer pack ice limit
- •• Winter pack ice limit
- ➤ Warm current
- ➤ Cool current

Currents and gyres

Ocean currents within the 10 percent of water closest to the surface have a noticeable effect on Earth's climate. The causes of currents and gyres (circular currents) are complex, and include water temperature and density, air pressure and temperature, wind direction and strength, gravity, land locations, and the rotation of Earth on its axis.

Gyre formation

The North Atlantic and South Atlantic gyres are two of the five major gyres that exist. The natural flow of currents away from the equator are affected by Earth's rotation. This is known as the Coriolis effect. In the Northern Hemisphere, gyre currents curve in a clockwise loop. In the Southern Hemisphere, the rotation is counterclockwise.

North Atlantic Gyre

South Atlantic Gyre

Climate Change and the World's Oceans

The ocean directly absorbs much of the atmosphere's rising heat, playing a vital role in climate change. It also absorbs increasing amounts of the greenhouse gas carbon dioxide.

The consequences of a warmer and more acidic ocean are being closely monitored and have been found to be harmful to marine life generally. Scientists are now researching methods of slowing the increasing acidity.

1 Healthy coral

2 Bleached coral

3 Dead coral

Coral bleaching

Increasing seawater temperatures cause the number of tiny colored algae, or zooxanthellae, that live within coral polyps to decline and then to lose their color. This results in only the white calcite skeleton being seen.

RISING ACIDIFICATION

Shellfish are members of a group of organisms known as marine calcifiers. Growth of their hard calcium carbonate shells for bodily protection requires slightly alkaline water. As more carbon dioxide is absorbed, seawater becomes more acidic. This results in weaker and thinner shells, leading to reduced numbers of shellfish.

Clam

Mussel

Mud whelk

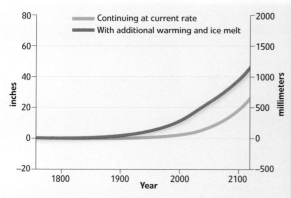

Future sea level rise

Higher temperatures cause waters to expand and sea levels to rise. A sustained increase in global temperature will also cause more glaciers and ice sheets surrounding the North Pole and across Antarctica to melt, with their water flowing into the ocean.

Deep-sea hatchet fish

Global warming most obviously affects the uppermost water zone. Since marine ecosystems are interconnected, marine life in deep water and on the seafloor are also threatened by issues such as acidification.

Warm, surface current
Salty, dense water plunges to the depths.

Great ocean conveyor

The conveyor is a global current system driven by water density differences. It is also known as thermohaline (temperature-salinity) circulation. Effects of global warming may include the inflow of less-dense ice melt from Greenland, reducing downwelling in the North Atlantic.

Cold, deep current
A turbulent mix of ocean waters circulates.

Marine Scientists

M arine scientists work in the largest research laboratory on Earth—the ocean. They study the sea and its interactions with the atmosphere, land, and ocean floor. This information is then used by governments, universities, and environmental organizations. Marine science is carried out at many locations and uses diverse and continually advancing processes and equipment.

Control room
The ROV (Remotely Operated Vehicle) control room is shipboard, and staffed by a pilot, navigator, scientists, and technicians who operate the ROV hundreds of feet (m) below the ship.

Taking water samples
Based on a small boat, marine technicians bottle water samples collected at various depths at specific locations. Water properties are tested using a CTD (conductivity, temperature, depth) device.

Tagging elephant seals
Until recently, elephant seals led a life of mystery. Nowadays, marine zoologists carefully glue tags to resting seals. These devices record the animals' journeys and are removed within 12 months.

Releasing seals
Seals are hunted for their fur. Also, their habitat is sea ice, which is declining in some areas. Scientists are joining conservationists in rescuing endangered seals and releasing them into safer waters.

Core sampling
A marine geologist uses a submersible hydraulic core sampler to obtain valuable information from below the ocean floor. Subtle clues are then used to understand the marine life from long ago.

Current Research

Significant research is being conducted to see how oceans will respond to global warming. Other research is being undertaken to see how oceans might be used to provide renewable and sustainable energy. Scientists also study certain sea creatures to understand the impact various human activities may have in the future.

1

2

3

1 Sea otter
These intelligent mammals live on the shores of the northern Pacific Ocean. Once almost extinct, they are currently on the threatened species list.

2 Sockeye salmon
Researching the feeding habits of sockeye salmon involves catching them and studying the contents of their stomach.

3 Phytoplankton
Using iron sulfate to encourage phytoplankton can potentially reduce atmospheric carbon dioxide but its use is controversial.

4 Logging non-native lionfish
Lionfish are a tropical, invasive species, whose numbers are being monitored off the southeast coast of the US.

4

Undersea Technology

U nderwater exploration has historically been conducted from within manned submersibles. They used scientific instruments that were designed to sample, observe, monitor, and record the underwater world. Newer technology allows for remote operation of underwater instruments. Devices can also be attached to animals and transmit images and information via satellite to researchers.

In both cases, the instruments need to withstand the corrosive, pressurized, and often pitch-dark environment.

Deep-diving *Alvin*

In operation since 1964, *Alvin* was the first deep-sea submersible that could carry a pilot and two observers. It can resist pressures down to 14,760 feet (4,500 m), and is equipped with a variety of monitoring, recording, and retrieval equipment. Its capability will improve once the most recent of a series of overhauls is completed.

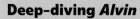

Hydrophone

A hydrophone is a computerized, acoustic microphone that is used to record underwater sounds. Hydrophones can be used with global positioning system (GPS) devices to track the movement of whales and other vocal marine animals.

ROV Hercules

Hercules is a remotely operated vehicle (ROV) attached by a long fiber-optic cable to its mother ship, where the pilot operates its controls. It is equipped with scientific instruments, video cameras, and manipulator arms. Hercules's motors provide thrust to move it in all directions, or allow it to hover.

Undersea glider AUV

Autonomous underwater vehicles (AUVs) exist in many different styles and are designed to operate independently. They are often powered by battery-operated propellers. Gliders are special AUVs that self-propel by changing their buoyancy. They are torpedo shaped, use wings and a rudder, and move by rising upward and then gliding forward. Unlike conventional AUVs, they are able to collect a mass of information over many months and across long ranges of distance.

A Healthy Planet

In the past, the ocean had been considered an endless resource, its vastness mistaken for a dumpsite. Scientists studying various marine environments have been calling the world's attention to its condition, and the importance of a healthy ocean is becoming widely accepted.

The intimate relationship between the ocean and planet Earth is significant. Excessive greenhouse gases and rising atmospheric and ocean temperatures are the focus of much scientific research. The task for marine and other scientists is to devise suitable means to avoid environmental catastrophes.

Blue whale
The gentle giants of the ocean, blue whales were hunted almost to extinction. Scientists report their distinctive blue whale song is now generally of lower pitch and volume. Thanks to increasing numbers, their calls only need to travel shorter distances.

CAUGHT BY LONGLINES

Longline fishing is a method that uses large, baited hooks and lines up to 60 miles (96 km) in length. Seabirds dive onto the hooks, become caught, and end up drowning. Other marine life also gets caught in the lines and becomes part of the bycatch.

Sharks caught in longlines

White harp seal
White harp seals feed on a variety of fish and are blamed for reducing the availability of fish for human consumption. Their fur is also valuable, and they are widely hunted. Too great a reduction in numbers, however, may disrupt the food chain and reduce commercial fish species farther.

Did You Know?

Global warming may be causing bird deaths. Because major upwelling currents are lessening, the number of krill near the water's surface is also becoming less. The result is mass starvation of seabirds.

Healthy coral growth

Coral is sensitive to small changes in water quality, so their healthy growth is indicative of a healthy ocean. Human activity can easily destroy this situation, and long-living corals in many reefs are in need of conservation.

Glossary

algae (AL-jee)
Simple, primitive marine plants.

autonomous
(aw-TAW-nuh-mus)
Independent, not subject to external control.

bacteria
(bak-TIR-ee-uh)
Single-cell microscopic organisms that reproduce by repeated cell division, and which may live and multiply without light or oxygen.

bioluminescence
(by-oh-loo-muh-NEH-sens)
A biological process within cells to produce light.

bycatch (BY-kach)
Unwanted marine species caught on hooks and nets which are used to catch other species.

calcite (KAL-syt)
Crystallized calcium carbonate.

calcium (KAL-see-um)
An elementary, metallic substance with abundant compounds.

carbon dioxide
(KAHR-bun dy-OK-syd)
A colorless gas used by plants in photosynthesis, and formed by decomposition of organic matter.

convection (kun-VEK-shun)
The movement of molecules of a hot material in a fluid that efficiently transfers heat.

core sampler
(KOR SAM-plur)
A drill with a hollow bit that extracts a cylindrical sample of underground material.

crustaceans
(krus-TAY-shunz)
Mainly aquatic animals with a hard external skeleton and no backbone.

crystalline (KRIS-tuh-lin)
A structure made up of distinct crystals.

density (DEN-seh-tee)
The ratio of the mass of a substance to its volume.

downwelling
(DOWN-wel-ing)
The downward movement of fluid, especially in the sea.

ecosystems
(EE-koh-sis-temz)
Systems within which living organisms interact with each other and their surrounding physical environment.

estuarine (ES-choo-wer-een)
Relating to the aquatic environment where rivers enter the ocean, mixing salt water and freshwater.

evaporation
(ih-va-puh-RAY-shun)
The conversion of a liquid into the vapor state.

glucose (GLOO-kohs)
A natural and abundant form of sugar that provides energy.

greenhouse gas
(GREEN-hows GAS)
Atmospheric gas that absorbs and traps heat from the Sun within Earth's atmosphere.

gyre (JYR)
Surface ocean currents that move in a circular motion.

habitat (HA-buh-tat)
The physical environment where a group of organisms lives.

hydrothermal
(hy-droh-THER-mul)
Relating to the action of heated water in Earth's crust.

impermeable
(ihm-PUR-mee-uh-bul)
Describes a material that prevents a liquid or gas passing through it.

lava (LAH-vuh)
Hot, molten rock at Earth's surface.

magma (MAG-muh)
Hot, molten rock within or below Earth's crust.

nutrients
(NOO-tree-ents)
Substances that are taken in by plants or animals to promote growth.

organic (or-GA-nik)
Matter derived from living organisms or based on carbon.

organism
(OR-guh-nih-zum)
A living system such as an animal, plant, fungus, or microorganism.

photosynthesis
(foh-toh-SIN-thuh-sus)
The process by which the Sun's energy is used, usually by plants, to produce carbohydrates, including sugars.

phytoplankton
(FY-toh-plank-tun)
Microscopic, usually single-cell marine plants.

plankton
(PLANK-tun)
Small organisms that drift in huge numbers near the ocean's surface and are a source of food for larger aquatic organisms.

plates (PLAYTS)
Geological rock structures of Earth's crust, often referred to as tectonic plates.

porous (POR-us)
Having a network of holes that allows liquids or gases to be absorbed or pass through.

predators
(PREH-duh-turz)
Animals that hunt other animals in order to live.

seepage (SEE-puj)
Liquid that has flowed or slowly passed through porous material.

seismic (SYZ-mik)
Relating to Earth vibrations associated with earthquakes.

shale (SHAYL)
Fine-grained, sedimentary rock formed in layers.

shock waves
(SHOK WAYVZ)
Moving locations of sharply increased pressure or density.

species (SPEE-sheez)
A group whose members have common attributes and can interbreed.

subduction
(sub-DUK-shun)
Forced movement of a tectonic plate down beneath a neighboring plate.

vents (VENTS)
Holes or cracks in Earth's crust from which lava and gases erupt.

Index

A

abyssal plains 14, 15
acidification 22
Alvin, submersible 26, 27
Antarctica 23
atmospheric circulation 20
autonomous underwater
      vehicle (AUV) 27

B

bacteria 18
bioluminescence 11, 12, 13
black smoker 17
blue whales 10, 28
blue-green algae 18
bycatch 28

C

continental shelves 14
coral atoll 6, 7
corals 6, 7, 22, 29
Coriolis effect 21

E

El Niño 20

G

gas 14
global warming 23, 25, 29
greenhouse gas 22, 28
Greenland 23
guyots 14, 15
gyres 21

H

hatchet fish 23
Hurricane Katrina 8
hurricanes 20
hydrophone 26

I

icebergs 6

K

krill 10, 29

L

La Niña 20
lava pillows 17
lionfish 25
longline fishing 28

M

magma 16
methane 14
mid-ocean ridge 14, 15
mucilage 18

N

natural gas 14
North Pole 23

O

oceanic trench 14, 15, 16
overfishing, commercial
      10, 11
ostracods 12

P

photosynthesis 7, 10
phytoplankton 7, 10, 18, 25
plastic pollution 18, 19
plates, tectonic 8, 15,16
power generation 9, 25

R

Remotely Operated Vehicle
      (ROV) 17, 24, 25
ROV Hercules 27

S

sea cucumbers 13
sea otters 25
shellfish 22

T

thermohaline circulation 23
tsunami, Asian 8

U

undersea glider AUV 27

V

viperfish 12
volcanoes 7, 14, 15

W

white harp seals 28

Z

zooplankton 10, 19

Websites

Due to the changing nature of Internet links, PowerKids Press has developed an online list of websites related to the subject of this book. This site is updated regularly. Please use this link to access the list:
www.powerkidslinks.com/disc/ocean